*NUNS ON A CHAIN GANG! ③
OR: THE NATURAL ANTIDEPRESSANT!
plus hundreds of other wacko "stuff" YOU NEVER-EVER see!!

by
ALAN M. RIPIN

ALSO BY THE AUTHOR
NUNS ON A CHAIN GANG!
NUNS ON A CHAIN GANG! ②
Movie Rights **STILL** Pending!

To order copies of this book, please visit
www.createspace.com/3899020
****

Contact the author for comments, etc.
at: aripin@verizon.net.
****

Copyright © 2012 Alan M. Ripin
All rights reserved.
ISBN: 1477600779
EAN13: 9781477600771

DEDICATION

TO ALL OF US WHO CAN APPRECIATE
THE SILLIER SIDE OF LIFE!

STOP! / RELAX! / TAKE A DEEP BREATH!

You're two(2) pages away from uncontrollable hysteria!!

CONTENTS

Wacko "stuff" #s 701 to #1,000 are within this masterpiece. *NOTE: Wacko "stuff" #1 to #340 can be found in "**NUNS ON A CHAIN GANG!**" published in 2010. Wacko "stuff" #341 to #700 can be found in "**NUNS ON A CHAIN GANG! ②**" published in 2011.

NUNS ON A CHAIN GANG ③

Wacko "stuff" you NEVER-EVER see!

701. HECK: the region where evil, but non-profanity users go after death

702. "Ben and Jerry" coming out of the closet and renaming their product line: "Dairy Queens"

703. A "swearing at" ceremony for all politicians

704. Goliath demanding a rematch from the "Valley of Elah Slingshot Commission"

705. Undertakers lobbying to legalize Driving While Intoxicated/ Driving While Texting/ and Driving While Using A cell phone

NUNS ON A CHAIN GANG ③

I CREATED THE CONCEPT! LET YOUR IMAGINATION DO THE REST!

ALAN M. RIPIN

706. Cement parachutes

707. Lincoln's Gettysburg Address: 1473 Main Street, Gettysburg, PA 17325

708. The Chairman of the Joint Chiefs of Staff going AWOL

709. A great white shark in a petting zoo

710. Anyone admitting that, "YES, a 3:18AM call really DID wake me up!"

Nuns on a chain gang ③

Wacko "stuff"
you NEVER-EVER see!

711. Walt Disney buying mouse traps

712. Congress officially changes the names of the United States Constitution, Bill of Rights, and the Declaration of Independence to the CONGRESSIONAL Constitution, etc., etc.

NUNS ON A CHAIN GANG 3

I CREATED THE CONCEPT! LET YOUR IMAGINATION DO THE REST!

713. The Hunchback of Notre Dame winning the Heisman Trophy

714. GOD's birth certificate

715. Vice-President Biden admits that he is the illegitimate son of a Zulu warrior

NUNS ON A CHAIN GANG ③

Wacko "stuff" you NEVER-EVER see!

716. The "Bridge Under The River Kwai"

717. Mandatory, hourly, lie detector tests for ALL politicians

718. "Moby Dick" politically corrected to "Moby Penis"

719. Wok Hudson, a gay Chinese chef

720. Grandma Moses chewing tobacco

*NUNS ON A CHAIN GANG!③

I CREATED THE CONCEPT! LET YOUR IMAGINA-TION DO THE REST!

721. "Standard & Poor's" downgraded to "Substandard & Destitute"

722. Burger King, under pressure from Tony Soprano, to change the name from "Whopper" to "The Italiano"

723. A vaccine for Beatlemania

724. A wheelchair-bound audience giving a standing ovation

725. AA meetings for Pre-Kindergarteners

NUNS ON A CHAIN GANG ③

Wacko "stuff"

YOU NEVER-EVER see!

726. A German deli: "For Better Or For Wurst"

727. A seller of shading products: "Oh, What A Beautiful Awning"

728. Ringling Sisters Barnum and Bailey Circus

729. Bruce Wintersteen

730. An Oscar for "Best Location Catering Service"

NUNS ON A CHAIN GANG ③

I CREATED THE CONCEPT! LET YOUR IMAGINA- TION DO THE REST!

ALAN M. RIPIN

731. Prince William and Kate mooning the Queen

732. Hot snow

733. A "muscle car" doing push-ups

734. An x-rated Irish meal: Corned beef and cleavage

735. "Community Day" in Outer Mongolia

NUNS ON A CHAIN GANG ③

Wacko "stuff" you NEVER-EVER see!

ALAN M. RIPIN

736. Buttered momcorn

737. "Happy Hours" at AA meetings

738. All New York City street signs printed only in braille

739. An ambidextrous halibut

740. Going out on a "visually-challenged" date

*NUNS ON A CHAIN GANG/3

I CREATED THE CONCEPT! LET YOUR IMAGINATION DO THE REST!

741. Shortgevity

742. Autumn fever

743. Revlon introduces Super king-sized lipstick for Ubangi women

744. "Death By Lethal Injection" – the award winning musical comedy

745. A "no-ring" alarm clock for insomniacs

*NUNS ON A CHAIN GANG/③

Wacko "stuff" you NEVER-EVER see!

746. A "left-hand" man

747. Honorees being present to receive posthumous awards

748. Superman retiring to an assisted living community

749. An Alzheimer patient playing "Hide and Seek"

750. Orthodox Jewish Catholics

NUNS ON A CHAIN GANG ③

I CREATED THE CONCEPT! LET YOUR IMAGINA- TION DO THE REST!

751. "Hebrew National" pork products

752. A fully loaded 18-wheeler overtaking a Porsche Cayman on a hill

753. A chain of Safari Tour Companies in Antartica

754. Any survey that truly addresses your concerns and leaves you with the feeling that your responses will make a difference

755. A school superintendent with just one key

NUNS ON A CHAIN GANG ③

Wacko "stuff" you NEVER-EVER see!

756. A "girl Wednesday"

757. Mouse droppings in the White House Oval Office

758. Politically corrected title: "Grimm's Gay Tales"

759. People NEVER complaining about the weather

760. Guinness "slim"

NUNS ON A CHAIN GANG (3)

I CREATED THE CONCEPT! LET YOUR IMAGINATION DO THE REST!

ALAN M. RIPIN

761. A drunken "bachelor's bash" in Afghanistan

762. A twenty-third world country

763. Correspondence in which "Dear", "Sincerely yours", "With Warm Regards", etc, etc, are meant literally

764. The day before hangover

765. A cold fudge sundae

NUNS ON A CHAIN GANG 3

Wacko "stuff" you never-ever see!

766. TOBACCO: The Miracle Drug

767. "Haitian Airways"

768. An Hasidic NFL strong safety

769. An ice cream omelet

770. A hate seat

*NUNS ON A CHAIN GANG/③

I CREATED THE CONCEPT! LET YOUR IMAGINATION DO THE REST!

ALAN M. RIPIN

771. A nun dealing blackjack in Las Vegas

772. A twenty-two deck luxury liner with one dining room that seats five

773. Yom Kippur and Thanksgiving falling on the same day

774. A senior assisted living complex on the summit of Mt. Everest

775. A wedding ceremony where the bride is given away (happily) by her ex

NUNS ON A CHAIN GANG ③

Wacko "stuff"

YOU NEVER-EVER see!

776. The President's limo pulled over and ticketed for DWI

777. Recycled toilet tissue

778. A "No Spitter": A major league baseball game during which no pitcher spits on the mound

779. A "Cattle Crossing" sign on Fifth Avenue and Forty-Second Street, NYC

780. A jet fighter landing on a submarine deck

NUNS ON A CHAIN GANG! ③

I CREATED THE CONCEPT! LET YOUR IMAGINA- TION DO THE REST!

781. A Rastafarian with a heavy Jewish accent

782. A hippopotamus nesting in a tree

783. New legal document replacing a divorce decree: a "Declaration of Independence"

784. A witch doctor doing his residency at the Mayo Clinic

785. A cadaver chewing bubble gum

NUNS ON A CHAIN GANG ③

Wacko "stuff" YOU NEVER-EVER see!

786. Royalty dining on "Spam"

787. Historians reveal that Lady Godiva was, in fact, Paul Revere in drag

788. An uncivil war

789. Congress passing legislation to add six additional letters to the alphabet

790. Personalized t-shirts with the wearers full social security number on the front and back

*NUNS ON A CHAIN GANG/③

I CREATED THE CONCEPT! LET YOUR IMAGINATION DO THE REST!

791. The Garden of Eden closed for renovations till further notice

792. A do-it-yourself embalming kit

793. Islamic females wearing string bikinis

794. Saudi Arabia and Yemen passing gay marriage legislation

795. An NHL hockey team on which ALL players have the surname: Jones, Smith, Brown, and/or Johnson

*NUNS ON A CHAIN GANG/③

Wacko "stuff"
you NEVER-EVER see!

796. An automated "...your approximate waiting time is ..." estimate that comes within a decade of reaching your designated responder

797. A bar code for unruly drinkers

798. A nearsighted rattlesnake attempting to mate with a garden hose

799. A sadistic cherub

800. A newborn with dentures

NUNS ON A CHAIN GANG ③

I CREATED THE CONCEPT! LET YOUR IMAGINA- TION DO THE REST!

ALAN M. RIPIN

801. Knights of the hexagonal table

802. A weather forecaster saying: "There's a nip in the air" (esp. at Pearl Harbor)

803. Zimbabwe weekly sweepstake prizes: One winning number (15 trillion dollars); Two winning numbers (100 trillion dollars)

804. An F-35 Lightning jet fighter skywriting

805. Vatican City chosen to host the 2018 Winter Olympics

NUNS ON A CHAIN GANG ③

Wacko "stuff" you NEVER-EVER see!

ALAN M. RIPIN

806. A flat chested diva

807. A magic carpet with two flight attendants and a sky marshal

808. An elephant with a nose job

809. A parade where the full band, not just the drums, is playing as they pass you

810. Japanese tourists without a camera

NUNS ON A CHAIN GANG ③

I CREATED THE CONCEPT! LET YOUR IMAGINATION DO THE REST!

811. A "Presidential Suite" in a flophouse

812. The law firm of "Dillinger, Gotti, and Capone, ESQ.

813. A drawbridge in the Sahara Desert

814. An uncle-eater

815. Hobos riding the "Orient Express"

NUNS ON A CHAIN GANG ③

Wacko "stuff" you NEVER-EVER see!

816. Aircraft de-icing at El Azizia (Africa) airport

817. A mezuzah posted on the door of the Sistine Chapel

818. A "scrolling electronic ticker" parade up the canyons of lower Broadway to City Hall

819. Group therapy for "gender confused" fetuses

820. A sadistic grief counselor

*NUNS ON A CHAIN GANG/3

I CREATED THE CONCEPT! LET YOUR IMAGINATION DO THE REST!

ALAN M. RIPIN

821. A dating service for terrorists

822. "Big Ben" converted to digital

823. A fully automated broomwash for affluent witches

824. General Custer's defective dreamcatcher

825. "NUNS ON A CHAIN GANG! #3,456"

NUNS ON A CHAIN GANG ③

Wacko "stuff" you NEVER-EVER see!

826. New dietary penal code: All inmates are required to eat two (2) square and one (1) rectangular meals per day

827. A celibate rabbit

828. The "Tooth Fairy" named Grand Marshal of the National Gay Pride Parade

829. The Hunchback of Notre Dame winning the "Mr Universe" contest

830. Fidel Castro wins the Mayor of Miami election in a landslide victory

NUNS ON A CHAIN GANG 3

I CREATED THE CONCEPT! LET YOUR IMAGINA- TION DO THE REST!

831. A men's room in a convent

832. NATO and the UN replaced by NYC's Guardian Angels

833. Niagara Falls going drip, drip, drip

834. Kremlin public relations photos showing Putin knitting baby caps

835. Jimmy Stewart fast-talking

NUNS ON A CHAIN GANG ③

Wacko "stuff" YOU NEVER-EVER see!

836. "Nazi Youth Cookies" annual fund raising campaign

837. "Postage Due" email

838. A social director on a slave ship

839. A serious hypochondriac named to head the FDA

840. Field, executive, and luxury box seats at the Roman Colosseum

*NUNS ON A CHAIN GANG/③

I CREATED THE CONCEPT! LET YOUR IMAGINATION DO THE REST!

841. Canned fruit cocktail in which you can taste the difference between the peaches, pineapples, pears, grapes, and cherries

842. The Mayflower finishing a distant second in the "America's Cup" race

843. New Jersey Governor, Chris Christie diagnosed with acute anorexia

844. New York Post headline: "CATEGORY 5 HURRICANE RELOCATES STATUE OF LIBERTY TO BOSTON HARBOR!"

845. "A Cannibal's Guide To Cooking" featuring finger food presentations

NUNS ON A CHAIN GANG ③

Wacko "stuff" you never-ever see!

846. A four year old Japanese prodigy performing Beethoven's "Moonlight Sonata" on the cymbals

847. Venus deMilo juggling

848. State troopers patrolling in pink, VW Beetle convertibles

849. Funeral home gift certificates

850. Adam's Mothers Day card returned with notation: "Unable To Locate"

NUNS ON A CHAIN GANG! ③

I CREATED THE CONCEPT! LET YOUR IMAGINATION DO THE REST!

851. Your own obituary

852. Baby Jesus opening Christmas presents

853. An oxygenius

854. A butler serving a diplomatic state dinner with his trousers on backwards

855. "The Elmer Fudd Institute Of Speech Therapy"

NUNS ON A CHAIN GANG ③

Wacko "stuff" you NEVER-EVER see!

856. Juliet and Romeo

857. Short John Silver

858. Tragedy Clubs: Where folks can go to have a good cry

859. A seventeen horse photo finish at the Kentucky Derby

860. Roses aren't red, violets aren't blue

"NUNS ON A CHAIN GANG" (3)

I CREATED THE CONCEPT! LET YOUR IMAGINA- TION DO THE REST!

ALAN M. RIPIN

861. A colorblind school crossing monitor

862. An illegal secretary

863. A hot air balloon breaking the sound barrier

864. The "Mormon Tabernacle Choir" downsizing to a duet

865. An erotic sandwich: Peanut butter and "KY" jelly

NUNS ON A CHAIN GANG ③

Wacko "stuff" you NEVER-EVER see!

866. 2077 Headline: "MAN LANDS ON THE SUN-OUCH!"

867. Mona Lisa snarling

868. Three pounds of flesh

869. An obese skeleton

870. ALL prices permanently returning to what they were ten years ago

*NUNS ON A CHAIN GANG/ ③

I CREATED THE CONCEPT! LET YOUR IMAGINATION DO THE REST!

ALAN M. RIPIN

871. Readable film credits

872. An illiterate book reviewer

873. Prescription drug names that can be correctly pronounced and/or spelled

874. The "Headless Horseman" sunbathing at a topless beach

875. N.Y. Giant coach, Tom Coughlin demanding a referee's review of a N.Y. Giant winning touchdown

*NUNS ON A CHAIN GANG/3

Wacko "stuff" you never-ever see!

876. The sun rising in the Southwest and setting in the Northeast

877. Genitalia: sexual organs of Italian males and females

878. Double-jointed cockroaches

879. The Salvation Coast Guard meetings

880. Spartacus elected into the "Gladiator's Hall Of Fame" on first ballot

*NUNS ON A CHAIN GANG! ③

I CREATED THE CONCEPT! LET YOUR IMAGINATION DO THE REST!

ALAN M. RIPIN

881. Japanese food anthem: If you knew sushi like I know sushi, oh, oh, ya, ya, ya, ya

882. An astronaut with acrophobia

883. A hobo playing an oboe

884. "IBS" (Irritable Bowel Syndrome) renamed to "PITA" (Pain In The Ass)

885. A touch football league for untouchables

NUNS ON A CHAIN GANG ③

Wacko "stuff" you NEVER-EVER see!

886. An igloo with a thatched roof

887. Wampum replacing the U.S. dollar as the official currency

888. Heterosexual marriages between illegal immigrants declared unconstitutional in Arizona

889. Santa Claus' dark side

890. Cell phones that self-destruct if heard by other than the user

*"NUNS ON A CHAIN GANG"(3)

I CREATED THE CONCEPT! LET YOUR IMAGINATION DO THE REST!

ALAN M. RIPIN

891. "Death By Lethal Injection": the new musical comedy

892. Watched water boiling

893. Alternate side parking restrictions suspended in the Sahara Desert

894. A toothless root canal specialist

895. A Royal Family seder

NUNS ON A CHAIN GANG ③

Wacko "stuff" you NEVER-EVER see!

896. Any toddler who doesn't go "bananas" when they see or hear a moving train

897. The "Tea Party's" nickname: "Chock full o'Nuts"

898. Sign on racist, segregated roadway: "DO NOT PASS!"

899. The "Budweiser Clydesdales" outsourced to India for cheaper feed

900. Clark Kent doing the "12-Step Program"

*NUNS ON A CHAIN GANG/③

I CREATED THE CONCEPT! LET YOUR IMAGINATION DO THE REST!

ALAN M. RIPIN

901. Chopsticks made in the USA

902. A part time gladiator

903. The highest paid "matinee idol" successful in his quest to be a waiter

904. Bears taking "NoDoz"

905. A slow-talking auctioneer

NUNS ON A CHAIN GANG ③

Wacko "stuff" you NEVER-EVER see!

906. Bottled drinking water turning sour

907. A "pork roast" fund-raising dinner at Temple Beth Israel

908. A dermatologist asking a patient: "How's your rash?"

909. A "red-light district" in a leper colony

910. Retired pilgrims collecting Social Security benefits

*NUNS ON A CHAIN GANG 3

I CREATED THE CONCEPT! LET YOUR IMAGINATION DO THE REST!

91. "Sammy Weinstein's Irish Pub"

92. Certified, return receipt requested, blackmail

93. Five Afghans who can spell "onomatopoeia" backwards while eating shredded wheat.

94. The long-term, overall effect human flatulence has on global warming

95. New shopping days following Thanksgiving: "Black Friday", "Latino Saturday", "Asian Sunday", and "Non-Denomination Monday"

*NUNS ON A CHAIN GANG/3

Wacko "stuff" you NEVER-EVER see!

ALAN M. RIPIN

916. Lepers celebrating Thanksgiving Day

917. A gay and lesbian hermaphrodite

918. Santa, awaiting sentencing, admits to dealing in child pornography

919. Spiders paying for websites

920. Topless pizza

NUNS ON A CHAIN GANG! ③

I CREATED THE CONCEPT! LET YOUR IMAGINATION DO THE REST!

921. A magic carpet with four (4) emergency exits

922. Thruway/Motorway "Rest Stops" renamed: "Easy-Piss"

923. A wigwam with aluminum siding

924. Carbonated waterbeds

925. Union delegates representing snake charmers

NUNS ON A CHAIN GANG ③

Wacko "stuff" you never-ever see!

ALAN M. RIPIN

926. Chariots with anti-lock brakes

927. Monogrammed ice cubes

928. Designer armor

929. Sunburned teeth

930. A great white guppie

NUNS ON A CHAIN GANG ③

I CREATED THE CONCEPT! LET YOUR IMAGINATION DO THE REST!

931. Siamese twins meeting for the first time at age 18

932. Manischewitz pork products

933. The word, "Antidisestablishmentarianism" featured in a love ballad

934. People living to age 115 experiencing peer pressure

935. Buddha named the winner of "The Biggest Loser"

NUNS ON A CHAIN GANG ③

Wacko "stuff" you never-ever see!

936. An octopus on crutches

937. The Iranian Presidential Inaugural Ball held at the local "Hooters"

938. A reality show featuring dry cleaner personnel called: "Meet The Presser"

939. Uncooked linguini sandwiches

940. A highly suspenseful "Whodunit" with the startling conclusion printed in

Sanskrit

NUNS ON A CHAIN GANG (3)

I CREATED THE CONCEPT! LET YOUR IMAGINA- TION DO THE REST!

941. A hypochondriac is named to head the FDA

942. A community college wins the Rose Bowl

943. A "wing-walker" performs on a supersonic jet

944. "Beano" and "Gas-X" gift certificates

945. The "National Enquirer" headline: "Jimmy Olson accuses Clark Kent

of Improper Sexual Advances!"

NUNS ON A CHAIN GANG ③

Wacko "stuff" YOU NEVER-EVER see!

946. Designer loincloths

947. Wasabi flavored cough drops

948. "Bingo Nite" at a brothel

949. Crematoriums offering a discount special on Ash Wednesday

950. President Ahmadinejad hosting a bagel and lox prayer breakfast

NUNS ON A CHAIN GANG 3

I CREATED THE CONCEPT! LET YOUR IMAGINATION DO THE REST!

951. Hitler wearing dreadlocks

952. A nuclear sub surfacing in NYC's Central Park lake

953. A dyslexic Braille instructor

954. Home schooling for brain surgeons

955. Augusta National Golf Club, home of the Masters Tournament, is purchased by N.O.W. for an undisclosed price

NUNS ON A CHAIN GANG ③

Wacko "stuff" you never-ever see!

956. A black female North Korean "Dear Leader"

957. A Muslim bar mitzvah

958. Disposable headstones

959. Locksmith workshops for incarcerated felons

960. "Smokey The Bear" doing time for arson

*NUNS ON A CHAIN GANG! ③

I CREATED THE CONCEPT! LET YOUR IMAGINATION DO THE REST!

961. A peanut butter and jellyfish

962. Shivering polar bears

963. A cavewoman with a nose job

964. Bumper cars with GPS

965. The Pillsbury Doughboy pigging out on Twinkies

NUNS ON A CHAIN GANG ③

Wacko "stuff" YOU NEVER-EVER see!

966. A fireworks spectacular scheduled for 2PM

967. A violent sandstorm in London's Trafalgar Square

968. A do-it-yourself sushi bar

969. Rabbis moonlighting as Chinese waiters

970. Alaskan champagne

NUNS ON A CHAIN GANG ③

I CREATED THE CONCEPT! LET YOUR IMAGINATION DO THE REST!

971. Goldfish melt sandwiches

972. A wasp wearing a yellow jacket

973. Noah diagnosed with double-vision

974. A line that moves faster than the line you left

975. A Chinese restaurant that serves rolls and butter with meals

NUNS ON A CHAIN GANG ③

Wacko "stuff" YOU NEVER-EVER see!

976. Yiddish speedwriting

977. A short-sleeved shirt with cufflinks

978. A new gay musical: "Guys and Guys"

979. Alice B. Toklas style "Similac" baby formula

980. George Washington admitting that he chopped down the cherry tree with a chainsaw

NUNS ON A CHAIN GANG ③

I CREATED THE CONCEPT! LET YOUR IMAGINATION DO THE REST!

981. A colonoscopy prep-kit called: "SH-T HAPPENS!"

982. A NYC sequel to "Downton Abbey": "Downtown Shabby: Life on the Bowery"

983. Pygmies doing the tango

984. X-rated bibles

985. Uptight pianos

NUNS ON A CHAIN GANG ③

Wacko "stuff" you NEVER-EVER see!

986. A cure for "Spring Fever"

987. Lip readers watching a movie on fast-forward

988. Gladiators staging a "walk-out" demanding improved wages, health benefits, and pensions

989. Asexual pick-up bars

990. Air Force One replaced by the Goodyear blimp

NUNS ON A CHAIN GANG! ③

I CREATED THE CONCEPT! LET YOUR IMAGINATION DO THE REST!

ALAN M. RIPIN

991. A colorless rainbow

992. Cuckoo clocks in a mental institute

993. A take-a-number machine at the door of the Oval Office

994. The October, 1985 Collector's Edition of "Playboy" in King Tut's tomb

995. A stupid old owl

NUNS ON A CHAIN GANG! ③

Wacko "stuff" you NEVER-EVER see!

996. A surgeon with practice limited to the removal of book appendixes

997. A "half-baked" sale

998. Paul Revere cited for TWH (texting whilst on horseback) and cautioning "The British Are Coming!"

999. Jimmy Hoffa's forwarding address

NUNS ON A CHAIN GANG ③

WACKO "STUFF" YOU NEVER-EVER SEE!

ALAN M. RIPIN

1000.

NUNS ON A CHAIN GANG! 4

Made in the USA
Columbia, SC
06 December 2021